COLORING & ACTIVITY BOOK

By Arsia Rozegar

Illustrated by Mike Amante

www.ShahnamehForKids.com

ISBN 9781677498352

FERDOWSI

ZAL AND SIMORGH

ROSTAM AND RAKHSH

GORDAFARID

SOHRAUB

THE FIGHT FOR FREEDOM

KEYUMARS, THE FIRST SHAH

DEEVS

HOOSHANG DISCOVERS FIRE

THE FLYING THRONE OF KAY KAVUS

SAUM

Search up, down, across, and diagonally for these!

ZAL	SAUM	SIMORGH
RUDABEH	ROSTAM	DAMAVAND
DEEV	HOJIR	SHAH
ALBORZ	PAHLAVAN	FERDOWSI
GORDAFARID	SISTAN	SOHRAUB

```
S  P  D  E  L  S  U  L  D  E  E  V  V  H
I  D  A  M  S  H  A  H  E  U  S  Y  G  O
S  O  M  L  H  A  G  U  G  X  I  Z  O  J
T  Y  A  C  B  C  S  H  M  Y  M  F  R  I
A  H  V  D  S  O  C  G  I  I  O  E  D  R
N  E  A  E  H  I  R  T  R  K  R  R  A  O
R  M  N  P  I  L  B  Z  A  L  G  D  F  Y
C  O  D  F  E  U  S  H  N  R  H  O  A  P
E  E  S  P  A  H  L  A  V  A  N  W  R  H
R  H  B  T  D  P  Z  T  W  E  M  S  I  P
Y  R  U  D  A  B  E  H  P  S  T  I  D  A
E  T  B  S  T  M  E  J  O  N  K  S  U  Q
X  A  S  O  H  R  A  U  B  E  S  H  E  M
```

KEYUMARS

SIAMAK

HOOSHANG

SIA DEEV

TAHMURAS

JAMSHID

ZAHAUK

KAVEH THE BLACKSMITH

FEREYDOON

FARRANAK

BARMAYOON AND KATAYOON

BARMAYEH

According to the Shahnameh, the Iranian New Year
Nowruz was founded by the great Shah Jamshid.

Can you name the 7 traditional items
found on a Nowruz Haftsin?

1.

2.

3.

4.

5.

6.

7.

Feel free to draw other items you
may find on a Nowruz Haftsin.

Answers:

1. Sabzeh (wheatgrass or lentil sprouts) 2. Samanu (sweet pudding) 3. Senjid (dried oleaster)

4. Seer (garlic) 5. Seeb (apple) 6. Sumagh (crushed spice) 7. Serkeh (vinegar)

CROSSWORD PUZZLE

DOWN
1. Who is commander of The White Fortress?
2. Who is Rostam's mother?
3. Who told Rostam where to find the Deevs?
5. Who is Gordafarid's father?
8. Who is Rostam's best friend?

ACROSS
4. What animal is found on Rostam's battle mace?
6. What is the tallest mountain in all of Greater Iran?
7. Who is the ruler of Turan?
9. What color is Zal's skin and hair?
10. Who is the mythical creature that raised Zal?

Answers:

1. Hojir 2. Rudabeh 3. Olaud 4. Ox 5. Gajdaham

6. Damavand 7. Afrasiyab 8. Rakhsh 9. White 10. Simorgh

SAUM

ZAL

ROSTAM

RAKHSH

GORDAFARID

Draw yourself as a Pahlavan from ancient times in Greater Iran.

KAY KAVUS

SEPID DEEV

AFRASIYAB

GORDAFARID

Help Zal find his way up to Simorgh in this mountainside maze.

ZAL AND SIMORGH

PRINCESS RUDABEH

MEHRAUB AND SINDOKHT

ARJANG DEEV

Unscramble these if you can!

1. MOSHRIG   _ _ _ _ _ _ _

2. NAHSAMSHE   _ _ _ _ _ _ _ _ _

3. VANDADMA   _ _ _ _ _ _ _ _

4. LAPHANAV   _ _ _ _ _ _ _

5. FOGRIDADAR   _ _ _ _ _ _ _ _ _ _

6. SMOTRA   _ _ _ _ _ _

7. HEDRAUB   _ _ _ _ _ _ _

8. MUSA   _ _ _ _

9. FAYIBARAS   _ _ _ _ _ _ _ _

10. HETINHAM   _ _ _ _ _ _ _

Answers:

1. Simorgh 2. Shahnameh 3. Damavand 4. Pahlavan 5. Gordafarid

6. Rostam 7. Rudabeh 8. Saum 9. Afrasiyab 10. Tahmineh

ARASH THE ARCHER

PRINCE SIAVASH

MOUNT DAMAVAND

Circle 7 things Rostam and Rakhsh encountered on their quest to rescue the Shah

SINGING SIREN

LAMB IN THE DESERT

LOKI

MINOTAUR

ENKIDU

SAURON

WITCH

WOLF

SEPID DEEV

ZAHAUK

UNICORN

LION

GIANT SPIDER

TIKOLOSHE

CYCLOPS

SIA DEEV

TALKING TREE

DRAGON

CTHULHU

ARJANG DEEV

SHARK

OLAUD

VAMPIRE

GRENDEL

CHUPACABRA

POLAR BEAR

Answers:

1. Lion 2. Lamb in the Desert 3. Dragon 4. Witch 5. Olaud 6. Arjang Deev 7. Sepid Deev

ROSTAM AND RAKHSH

ROSTAM BATTLES THE DRAGON

ROSTAM AND PRINCESS TAMINEH

ROSTAM OUTWITS AKHAVAUN DEEV

ROSTAM CLASHES WITH SOHRAUB

ROSTAM RESCUES BIJAN

ROSTAM TAKES AIM

Made in the USA
Middletown, DE
24 June 2023

33143429R00064